HOW TO GET LAND FOR FREE

The comprehensive guide

Kerr Rawden

Copyright © 2021 Kerr Rawden

All rights reserved

Contents

1. Introduction
2. What is adverse possession?
3. Finding appropriate land
4. Staking your claim
5. Living on and using your land
6. Getting the land in your name legally
7. Taxes and registration fees
8. Pro tips to aid the adverse possession process
9. Frequently asked questions
10. Conclusion
11. Resources

1. INTRODUCTION

A few months ago, I released a YouTube video detailing how I had found, and claimed as my own, a piece of unregistered land in Somerset, England - using the legal process of adverse possession. I was subsequently bombarded with questions, requests for more information and even consultancy offers from people who wanted to do the same thing.

The sheer volume of requests for more information and the overwhelming level of interest led me to the realisation that I needed to do more to disseminate this little-known but highly useful information. And so this book was born - a comprehensive guide of all the steps to claiming land in the UK. The information in it is a valid and legal method of acquiring such land through a process known as adverse possession. This guide designed to hold your hand all the way from a mild interest in this subject through to fully owning your own piece of land – which you got completely for free! There are some minor costs associated with the process (e.g. the cost of printing out a sign to claim the land etc), but the land itself will cost you nothing.

Adverse possession laws also exist in the USA, Canada, Australia, New Zealand and Ireland, and there are many more countries in which you can claim land by using this process. However, the examples with which I have experience, and which I will be highlighting in this book, relate to the position as it applies in the UK.

I will note that in Scotland, the process is known as 'Positive Prescription', rather than 'Adverse Possession' as it is known in England, Wales, Northern Ireland (and much of the rest of the world).

I will not litter this book with the confusing jargon and legal terminology that often comes with the territory. Instead, I will explain the processes and steps as simply and as thoroughly as I can, so they are understandable to all.

I truly hope this book will inspire as many people as possible to get out there, find some land and claim it as their own. This is the only option for many people to get on the property ladder, in an epoch where stagnant wages and mooning land prices have made it damn near impossible for a majority of the population to do so.

My ethos is to disseminate useful information and knowledge as widely as I can, to aid as many people as possible to achieve freedom and sovereignty in their lives.

'The system of private property is the most important guaranty of freedom, not only for those who own property, but scarcely less for those who do not.' – Fredrich August Hayek

2. WHAT IS ADVERSE POSSESSION?

Adverse possession is a legal principle under which a person who does not have legal title to a property (usually land) may acquire legal ownership of that property based on continuous possession or occupation, without the permission of its legal owner. Basically, adverse possession is a way for people to claim land as their own, without needing permission.

You will probably be aware that adverse possession is applicable to land under ownership, however, in this book we will focus primarily on using adverse possession to claim land that is unregistered and we believe to be unowned. This is for a few reasons.

Firstly, claiming land that is truly unowned is far more likely to produce positive results. If you know a plot of land is unowned there will be no chance of an owner appearing in a few years and trying to turf you out. It is also worth noting that The Land Registration Act of 2002 changed the adverse possession laws with regard to registered land, making it a lot easier for registered proprietors to prevent applications for adverse possession of their land being completed successfully. These new laws make adverse possession claims on registered land far more difficult, and an increasing number of claims on registered land are being rejected. The only situation in which I believe it is worth making an adverse possession claim on registered property is if you are in adverse possession of land adjacent to your owned property, mistakenly believing it to be yours. If the exact boundary of the properties has not been determined, and the estate has been registered for over a year, your adverse possession claim would more than likely be granted.

On a separate note, it is worth noting that if you are in adverse possession of registered land, and apply to be registered as proprietor after 10 years, the registered owner will be notified (so they can oppose the claim). The owner will likely oppose the claim (by serving a counter notice to the registrar) and your application will likely be rejected. However, this is where it gets interesting - if you remain in adverse possession of the property for a further 2 years, you can reapply to be registered as proprietor and this time your application will be accepted regardless of whether or not anyone opposes the application. So, if you can remain on the property for

2 more years despite your initial application being rejected, you are guaranteed to be granted adverse possession. This route would likely be one of hassle and conflict with the registered proprietor, so I would recommend simply going for land that is unregistered and preferably unowned.

That is the last I will speak of claiming *registered land,* as I believe it to be far more ethical to claim land that doesn't belong to someone, rather than land that does, regardless of whether it is being used or not. I'm not here to encourage the country to take up arms and place a bunch of claims on each other's land - I'm simply trying to provide an ethical way for the average person to acquire property that doesn't require the financial dominance required to get on the property ladder these days.

So, how does adverse possession work?

Well, to claim land by adverse possession, three essential principles must be fulfilled. Firstly, adverse possession requires factual or exclusive possession of the land, meaning you must fence off the area of the land as your own, if it's not already fenced off. Secondly, you must have an intention to possess the land - you must use the land for something, not just leave it abandoned for years. Thirdly, you must possess the land without consent - if you acquire land by asking someone else's permission, you are acknowledging that they own the land, which would obviously eradicate your claim to it. You must under no circumstances ever refer to the land as anything other than belonging to you. It is important to keep records of all works carried out, keep all invoices for materials used, take regular images with date and geo-location on, give receipts if you rent it out, keep the land in good condition and make friends with the locals to support your claim. We will go into this in more detail later on, but for now, let's focus on finding an appropriate piece of land.

3. FINDING APPROPRIATE LAND

So, first things first, we are going to want to find a piece of land. Taking the time to do your research on pieces of land at this stage is a vital step that will save you many headaches later on down the line. Naturally, there are a number of factors we need to consider when selecting a plot of land:

- Status of land (i.e. registered/unregistered/unowned)
- Utility of the land (can it be used for the desired purpose?)
- Restrictions on land (green belt, heritage sites, conservation areas etc)

The pecking order, as far as I'm concerned, would be to first check the status of the land. If it is registered, I would discard it. Some people may choose to place a claim on a piece of land that is registered (for example if it has been abandoned/disused for 12 years), but for me it represents too much hassle and potential confrontation, when there are plenty of legitimately unowned plots of land out there just waiting for you to swoop in! Also there is an ethical issue - I'm sure there are plenty of owned and abandoned plots of land it would be ethical to claim, but there are also plenty that would be unethical to claim and would feel more like stealing. Morality, however, is completely subjective, which leaves a huge grey area between the two concepts, which must be interpreted on an individual basis.

About 15% of the UK's land is unregistered, but only 3% is unowned. You will therefore want to collate a list of unregistered land that is viable for your desired use and do your research to check if it is truly unowned or not. A website I have found very useful for browsing unregistered land on a map is (www.map.WhoOwnsEngland.Org). This is one of the only free services for this purpose. You can scroll through the map function to find unregistered land in your local area. Jot down a few sites of interest, and you're ready to go and check them out in person!

Unfortunately, this map only shows the status of land in England and Wales, not for the rest of the UK, or any other countries. If you live outside of England and Wales however, do not despair, for there are other ways of finding unregistered land.

Scout your local area. Drive around looking for plots of land that look abandoned or disused. Rotten fence posts, rusty padlocks and rusty gates are often a good sign to look for. Once you have a few sites in mind, you can search for the title deeds on the land registry on the government website. You need the land specifics (i.e. the exact address or coordinates) to carry out the search, and each search costs £3. You can now discard the plots of land that are registered, and proceed to the next step with the unregistered plots. You may want to check the land out in person before searching for the title deeds, as you may want to discard some plots of land (if they aren't of use to you) before searching the land registry, saving yourself £3 per search.

Once I had a list of unregistered plots in my interested area, I would check them out in person and start doing a bit more in-depth research on them. This is where your desired land usage really comes into play. In this step you'll want to check the utility of the land, which is mostly a visual analysis. Can the land be used for the purpose we want it to? Is it on a slope? What's access like? Soil composition? Pests? Flood risk? Has planning permission already been granted? Is it near or in any protected or restricted areas? If you want to graze cattle, a chalky woodland probably isn't the right answer. If you want to live off-grid - you must think about practicalities like access to water and sewage disposal. If you want to grow vegetables, is the soil the right composition? If you want to bury treasure you'll need to make sure it's not in a flood plain that could wash it away forever!

Depending on your intended use of the land, some of these factors may be more important than others. You will consider different factors if you are trying to acquire some land on which to grow food compared to acquiring land where you intend to raise livestock, or live on. From here you can shortlist your final few candidates, based on suitability to your personal needs. You will also want to check whether the land is part of any protection orders - make sure it isn't in a green belt or heritage site that may affect what you want to do with the land.

These in-person site visits can be a great way to meet the locals and find out more details of the history of the land, including information about potential owners. In these visits, interactions with the locals could prove incredibly valuable. This is the best way of finding out if the land is truly unowned or simply unregistered, gives you an idea of the people in the local area, their attitudes towards the land and each other, and the viability of your claim. However, beware how much information you give to the locals you speak to. You may find some are hostile to your claim, and many would rather claim unowned land themselves than let someone else swoop in and take it if they find out what you are up to. Divulging your intention could prove a bit of a risky move, but there is also potential benefit in being forthcoming and upfront with the people in the surrounding area, as they can provide you with information you wouldn't otherwise discover.

Interacting with the locals is also one of the only real ways of finding out if the land is truly unowned or not before staking your claim - the local people's knowledge of the land will be far more detailed than anything you can find online.

I found my piece of land by being quite vocal about my intentions. I was talking to a farmer acquaintance of mine about my interest in adverse possession and desire to acquire some land when he told me about a piece of land he knew about on the peripheries of his land. He told me an old couple used to own it and lived there until they died. They died with no relatives or descendants, so the land went to ruin and their cottage slowly disintegrated over the years. It was mostly forested, so the farmers in the area had no real interest in it, as they couldn't raise livestock or grow crops on it at a scale large enough to be worth clearing the land. Nobody had ever stepped forward to claim it, so it just sat there disused. Knowing the history of the land like this meant I could be sure my claim would never be contested by a 'rightful owner' and so I figured it would be a great plot to claim.

So, now you have your final candidates. We know the land is unregistered, and is a suitable plot for your desired usage. We just want to do some final checks on the land. These can be done online or on the phone to the local council, and can be used to find out if the land is restricted in any way - i.e. if it lies in a green belt, conservation area, national park or heritage site. You will also want to find out if planning permission has already been granted to the plot.. If it hasn't already been granted, has anyone ever applied for planning permission on this land, and been rejected? If so, why was it rejected? If it was rejected for a similar usage to what you want to do, that could be a red flag. If it was rejected for an entirely different purpose, you could still stand a good chance. If nobody has ever applied for planning permission, you can speak to the local council or planning authority and get an idea of how likely it would be to be passed. As long as you tick the boxes with regard to planning permission and stick to the allowed specifications, you shouldn't have a problem being granted it.

Note that one does not need to be the legal owner of land to apply for planning permission. Once you place a claim on a piece of land, you can apply for planning permission straight away, there is no need to wait 12 years until the land is legally in your name.

If you can't find out whether a piece of land is truly unowned or simply unregistered, you can proceed with the first step of staking your claim to find out.

4. STAKING YOUR CLAIM

Once you have selected the piece of land on which you want to stake your claim, the best idea is the sign technique. Simply print out and laminate a sign saying 'Private property'. Put a telephone number on it too. Note that at this point, it would probably be worth buying an additional SIM Card and phone for the sole purpose of this. That way, if you get a call from an unknown number, you already know what it is going to be about.

Keep records of you making your claim. Take photos of you in your land, with your sign. If you make sure Geo-location and time-stamp settings are on, the images will save the location of the photos and the time and date in the meta-data of your pictures. This will serve as evidence of the date and location you originally claimed the land.

Leave the land for a few weeks, months even. If someone calls you up asking why the hell you've put a sign up on their land, you know that land is owned by someone. If the weeks trickle into months, and you hear no squeak, the coast looks a little clearer.

Of course, if you have done your due diligence into the land and have discovered that it is truly unowned (and trust the sources this information came from), then you need not bother putting your number on the sign (although you may still want to).

So, now we are actually staking a claim on the land, there are a number of requirements we need to make sure are ticked off.

Factual possession:
In Powell v McFarlane, ((1977) 38 P & CR 452. The House of Lords approved this statement of the law in J A Pye (Oxford) Ltd v. Graham [2002] UKHL 30.) Slade J said:

"Factual possession signifies an appropriate degree of physical control. It must be a single and [exclusive] possession, though there can be a single possession exercised on behalf of several persons jointly. Thus an owner of land and a person intruding on that land without his consent cannot both be in possession of the land at the same time. The question of what acts constitute a sufficient degree of exclusive physical control must depend on the circumstances, in particular the nature of the land and the manner in which land of that nature is commonly used or enjoyed ... Everything must depend on the particular circumstances, but broadly, I think what must be shown as constituting factual possession is that the alleged possessor has been dealing with the land in question as an occupying owner might have been expected to deal with it and that no one else has done so."

Where the land was previously open ground, fencing is strong evidence of factual possession, but it is neither indispensable nor conclusive.

In short, the above simply means you must fence off your land to establish factual possession, and use it as an owner would.

The intention to possess:
You must show an intention to possess the land, to put it to use. You can do anything legal with the land - you could put livestock on it, install beehives on it, grow crops on it or you could live on it (more on that later).

A great tip I have heard on the grapevine is to install bee-hives on the land. Keeping bees on the land, particularly if you are harvesting honey, is an excellent way to show an intention to possess and use the land. Bees are also great for local ecosystems and the local flora, and show you are taking care of the land.

Work you may do on the land can also show an intention to possess - i.e. clearing undergrowth, landscaping, building. Keep photographic evidence of the works you carry out, which will support your claim.

Possession without the owner's consent:

Possession is never 'adverse' within the meaning of the 1980 Act if it is enjoyed under a lawful title. Obviously, if you have asked a land-owner's permission to be on their land, you are recognising that they own the land, and it therefore cannot possibly be yours. As soon as you acknowledge someone else's ownership of the land, your claim becomes void.

Restrictions:

There are some restrictions that can prevent people claiming adverse possession in certain circumstances.

The following circumstances, taken from the UK government website, prevent an application being made for registration based on adverse possession, but are unlikely to apply to anyone reading this book:

- the registered proprietor is an enemy or detained in enemy territory, or has been an enemy or detained in enemy territory in the 12 months before the date of the application (Schedule 6, paragraph 8(1) of the Land Registration Act 2002)
- the registered proprietor is unable because of mental disability to make decisions about issues of the kind to which an application for adverse possession would give rise, or is unable to communicate such decisions because of mental disability or phys-

ical impairment (Schedule 6, paragraph 8(2) of the Land Registration Act 2002)
- the squatter is a defendant in proceedings which involve asserting a right to possession of the land, or judgment for possession has been given against them in the last 2 years (Schedule 6, paragraph 1(3) of the Land Registration Act 2002)
- the estate in land was held on trust at any time during the period of 10 years ending on the date of the application, unless the interest of each of the beneficiaries in the estate was an interest in possession (Schedule 6, paragraph 12 of the Land Registration Act 2002)
  - arguably this means that an application cannot be made where, at any point during this period, the registered proprietor at the time (i) was dead and their estate was being administered, (ii) was bankrupt and their property was being administered by the trustee in bankruptcy or (iii) (being a company) was being wound up. In each of these cases the registered estate is subject to a form of trust (Ayerst v C & K (Construction) Ltd [1976] A.C. 167)

So, now we have staked our claim on our new plot of land, what can we do with it?

5. LIVING ON AND USING YOUR LAND

There are a number of things to think about when it comes to living on your land, the most important being what are you going to live in, and do you need planning permission? Well, there are a number of ways to live on land without planning permission, but for some dwellings you will need planning permission. I will split these into 3 categories - mobile/temporary structures, permanent non-residential buildings, and permanent residential buildings.

Mobile structures

Mobile structures are a great way to live on the land without planning permission. A mobile structure will typically have wheels attached and can be moved. Shepherd's huts, caravans, converted vans and tiny houses on trailers are all great examples of mobile accommodation. You can place these on the land, but are technically only supposed to live there a maximum of 28 days a year. However, this doesn't seem to be enforced across the UK for people living on their own (claimed or otherwise) land. I have found plenty of cases of people being moved on from other people's land, after complaints by the owners - but on your own land, with nobody to complain about your presence, it may not be something anyone even notices, let alone has a problem with. I know plenty of people who live in a mobile home permanently on claimed land, and have never had a problem. This is another reason it is so important to do your due diligence and make sure the land you are claiming is truly unowned.

I have spoken to people who have even put a shipping container on land, and welded wheels to the bottom. These wheels do not function, yet seem to still classify the container as a temporary or mobile structure. This appears to have worked for quite a few people, and there is barely any scrutiny on matters like this, although this loophole may not be the most reliable approach, as a pedantic observer could easily argue it isn't actually mobile. A counter argument to this would be that shipping containers can be moved on the back of a lorry relatively easily, and are therefore mobile structures.

You can build certain permanent structures and do certain work on land without planning permission. These are known as permitted developments, and are derived from a general planning permission, granted not by the local council authority but by parliament. In some parts of the UK, generally known as 'designated areas' permitted development rights are more restricted. For example, if the land is:

- a Conservation Area
- a National Park
- an Area of Outstanding Natural Beauty
- a World Heritage Site or
- the Norfolk or Suffolk Broads.

Claiming land in one of the above designated areas comes with many challenges aside from building structures, so it's important to make sure you check the status of the land before claiming it. I would not be claiming any land classified as any of the above.

If you are unsure, contact your local planning authority and discuss your proposal before any work begins. They will be able to inform you of any reason why the development may not be permitted and if you need to apply for planning permission for all or part of the work.

Permanent non-residential buildings

A range of buildings can be erected without normal planning permission, usually for the purposes of forestry or agriculture.

Forestry

Forestry is the craft of creating, managing, using, conserving and repairing forests and woodlands. If the land you have claimed is in a forest or wooded area, either fully or partly, you could use this to your advantage. The range of forest buildings that can be erected without normal planning permission include the erection, extension or alteration of a forestry building, such as a tool shed, store, office, shelter, or putting in an access track. These are referred to as Permitted Developments (PD). The nitty gritty intricacies of these developments are in Part 7 of the General Permitted Development Order 1995 (GDPO).

To fall under a Permitted Development for forestry, the building or track must be used primarily for the purposes of forestry, as opposed to for leisure, educational activities or residence. There are no restrictions on the size of the forestry building (there are for agricultural Permitted Development rights). There are no requirements that the forestry must be run as a trade or business - so you would be well within your rights to build a Permitted Development for forestry as a hobby. Full Permitted Development rights apply to any size of forestry holding (for full agricultural Permitted Developments, your land must be over 5 hectares). There is no stipulation that it must relate solely to forestry - it can be used for other purposes as long as forestry is the main purpose.

To qualify as a Permitted Development for forestry, an erected building cannot be used as a permanent dwelling, cannot be within 25 metres of a classified road, and must be 'reasonably necessary' for the purposes of forestry. Buildings must be designed for the purposes for which they are intended - so you couldn't build a residential mansion and claim it is a Permitted Development for forestry.

A condition of Permitted Development rights for forestry is that you must notify the local planning authority of what you intend to do. Note - this is not an application for permission, it is merely a heads up. This involves filling in a simple form, including a map and drawing of the land. The planners then have 28 days in which to notify you that your development shouldn't begin without their prior approval of the siting, design and external appearance. They may ask for these details, but often don't. At this point they could also reject the proposal as not 'reasonably necessary' for the purposes of forestry - so it is important to plan this carefully.

A precedent set by one planning appeal (T/APP/V2255/A/97/286193/P7) provides a useful guide as to what can be erected in a woodland or forest. In this particular case, they allowed a 6 by 18 metre wooden building for the storage of equipment, as a workshop for producing fence posts and as an office with washroom facilities, all of which were considered necessary for managing a 21 hectare plot of woodland in Kent. This would be a great legal precedent to model your Permitted Development for forestry.

Using a caravan for forestry purposes (e.g. storage,

shelter for workers, office) would also be acceptable, providing the caravan is not for residential use, as it falls outside planning controls, so you would not need permission from a planning authority. According to the Caravan Sites Act 1968, the legal definition of a caravan includes mobile homes and self built structures. Under this definition, the caravan doesn't have to have wheels, as long as it is under the size limit (60 feet long, 20 feet wide and 10 feet high), can be delivered in no more than two sections by lorry, and is capable of being moved in one piece along a road when assembled.

Agriculture

For agricultural Permitted Developments, a two-tier system applies, with less generous Permitted Development rights applying to plots of land smaller than 5 hectares.

For plots of land larger than 5 hectares, Permitted Development rights apply as long as the building is not classed as a dwelling, it is used solely for the purpose of agriculture, it is not the first agricultural construction on the unit, it is less than 75 metres away from the nearest part of a group of principal farm buildings, it is more than 75 metres from any neighbouring house, it is less than 500 square metres and less than 12 metres in height, it is more than 9 metres from the middle of a road, and it is not the first agricultural construction on the land. So, unless you want to build something on claimed land adjacent to a farm you already own - agriculturally Permitted Developments are probably not a viable option for many of you reading this. For plots of land smaller than 5 hectares, the conditions are even more stringent.

There are a few different classes of Permitted Development Rights you can apply for, for small agricultural permitted developments:

- Class A: Allows development related to agricultural buildings (including for machinery and crop storage, for extension, erection or alteration, as long as it pertains to agriculture.
- Class O: Covers those who wish to change current agricultural buildings that are used as offices into houses or dwellings, as long as the structure is not a listed building, in a safety hazard zone, near a military storage area, near heritage or protected land and the office structure has been in place since before March 29th, 2013.
- Class Q: For turning agricultural buildings (not office type) into a house or dwelling. It allows for up to five dwellings (and up to 865 square metres of floor space) to be converted. The building must have already been in agricultural use since March 20th 2013, and

the new development cannot exceed the current external dimensions of the existing building, and it cannot be built in Areas of Outstanding Natural Beauty.
- Class R: For converting agricultural buildings into buildings with a purpose aside from dwellings (such as retail units, offices or leisure centres). The construction can't exceed 500 square meters on any single farm, applies to agricultural buildings in use since July 3rd 2012 and does not apply to areas near monuments, safety hazard areas, or military storage areas.
- Class S: Allows agricultural buildings to be converted to state-funded schools or registered nurseries.

Permanent residential buildings

For permanent residential dwellings (e.g. building a house) you usually need planning permission. The good news is that you can apply for planning permission on your claimed land before it is in your name legally - so no need to wait 12 years! You can apply for it on day one! It would be a good idea to check the history of the land before you claim it. An ideal plot of land to claim would be one for which planning permission has already been granted. It is often the case that a previous owner has been granted planning permission, but hasn't gone ahead and built anything. These plots will still have planning permission, and even if your proposed development is different to what has been granted permission, it may be easy to amend the slight differences and get it granted for what you desire.

You can check with the local council or authority for the history of the land. Perhaps someone has previously applied for planning permission and been rejected - this knowledge could render the land useless to you, depending what you want to do with it.

If nobody has ever applied for planning permission on the land, it could be useful to speak to the local council to assess your chances of having planning permission granted - and consider whether any conditions attached to the planning permission will affect what you want to do with the land.

It goes without saying that if you claim a piece of land that already has a building on it (e.g. a cottage), you don't need to apply for planning permission - however, any additional extensions you may want to build may require it.

6. GETTING THE LAND IN YOUR NAME LEGALLY

Getting the land in your name legally can take 12 years. This may seem like a long time (and it is!), but you will be able to start using the land, and even making money off it from the day you put your claim on it.

If you decide to make a bit of cash from the land (whether by renting it out, growing crops, livestock etc) but it turns out the land has an owner who comes and takes the land back off you, you still get to keep the cash you made off the land whilst you had claimed it. You wouldn't have to hand that over to the owner, although he may be able to keep anything you may have built on the land.

So, what's the process to get the land in your name?

After 5 years, you can apply for temporary ownership of the land. This doesn't mean a whole lot legally, but is a good way to strengthen your claim on the land, and gets the process moving in the direction you want it to. Your claim is usually considered stronger with temporary ownership than without. It could, however, alert potential owners to what you are trying to do much earlier - again highlighting the need to do your research and ensure the land is truly unowned.

After 10 years you can apply for full ownership of the land. This puts the land in your name legally, as long as nobody comes forward within 2 years of you applying for ownership. If the land does have an owner, they have these 2 years to come forward and *prove* they own the land. They must show the land's title deeds and proof of ownership to do so. This prevents people just trying to claim the land you have claimed. If nobody comes forward in these two years, you are registered as the land's proprietor. I have provided a link to the government website in the 'resources' section at the end of this book, where you can find the adverse possession application forms to fill in.

As I mentioned earlier, if someone *does* contest your claim, and prove they own the land, but don't kick you off, and you remain in adverse possession for a further 2 years, you can reapply for adverse possession of the land, and this time it will definitely be granted, even if the 'owner' tries to prevent it.

So, if all goes according to plan, it takes 12 years from placing your claim to having the land in your name legally. This may seem like an age, and it is, but you will be able to use the land and profit from it from day one.

The main downside of this 12 year wait is that people may not be willing to invest properly in the land (e.g. by building on it) if they aren't 100% sure someone isn't going to come and take the land back off them at some point. The 12 year wait can make people feel insecure about their claims, and fearful of taking a big loss should a legitimate owner one day appear. This is precisely why doing your due diligence is so important, to ensure the land is genuinely unowned.

7. TAXES AND REGISTRATION FEES

So, once the land is in your name, must you pay any taxes, stamp duty, or fees on it? Well, unfortunately nothing is completely free nowadays, so yes, a small fee will be due. Thankfully, the taxes paid on land acquired through adverse possession are substantially less than normal property purchases, and are only due once your adverse possession application has been successful and the land is officially in your name. The fee owed is dependent on the value of the land you have claimed, and at the time of publication of this book, go as follows for land acquired through adverse possession:

Value of property	Fee / Tax due (including adverse possession discount)
0 - £80,000	£30
£80,001 -	£60

£100,000	
£100,001 - £200,000	£140
£200,001 - £500,000	£200
£500,001 - £1,000,000	£400
£1,000,001+	£680

You will also need to pay an adverse possession registration fee of £70 for unregistered land, or £130 for registered land, when you file your application for adverse possession.

8. PRO TIPS TO AID THE ADVERSE POSSESSION PROCESS

Find a small plaque of lead and inscribe your name, personal details and the date you fenced the area. Have a witness add their details and ask them to accompany you when you bury it beneath one of your fence corner posts. This little known trade secret goes back a long way in history and has been known to help win the case if it comes to future legal contests. Nowadays, one could argue this is obsolete as we can time-stamp and add geolocation tags on photos taken with our smart phone, but none-the-less this could aid your claim, and certainly wouldn't harm it.

Build a beehive on your land - it is a super cheap and easy way to legitimise your claim, and shows your intent to possess and use the land, without requiring your constant presence.

A tip to finding unregistered land in a town is to look for huge trees that are blocking everyone's satellite signal. Phone your council explaining you'd like the trees managed/cut back to allow signal through to your house. The council will deny ownership of the land (if they don't own it, of course). They'll probably tell you to call somebody else, who may also deny ownership. If everyone denies ownership, you can put in a claim. If you obtain letters from all the alleged 'owners' who aren't really owners, confirming it isn't their land, then even better!

9. FREQUENTLY ASKED QUESTIONS

What about Scotland and Northern Ireland?
In Scotland it is virtually the same process, but it is called positive prescription rather than adverse possession. In Northern Ireland, it is the same as England and Wales.

What countries can one do this in?
There are so many countries with adverse possession laws, including Canada, the USA, Ireland, Australia, New Zealand, Russia, plenty of Europe and many more countries around the world.

When putting up a fence how do you know exactly where the border to that bit of land is exactly?
The title deeds for the surrounding plots should have maps with their boundaries on them. If the boundaries are not clear, or drawn at all, you have a bit more leeway to define the boundary yourself.

Doesn't land go to the crown if the owners die with no

descendents?
Technically, yes, but this is a mere technicality. Technically the crown still owns New Zealand and Australia! This has no effect on adverse possession claims.

Can I do this on land adjacent to my house?
Absolutely! In fact, if the land borders onto your house, it makes it far easier to build on it (whether your current planning permission allows it, or whether you need to apply for further planning permission), and you also can benefit from more Permitted Development rights.

If I find an abandoned house with land and I start using the land as my own, what do I do if someone comes on the land saying it belongs to them? Do they need to show me the deed to prove it's their land or do I just take their word for it?
Never take anyone's word for it. They could be lying through their teeth! I would simply say that the land is yours, end of story, saying as little as possible. If they insist, tell them to prove it by showing you the title deed. It is important to refer to the land as your own, if you infer in any way that the land could be owned by someone else, it can void your claim on it.

There's some unregistered land right next to our house which is owned by someone who keeps a shipping container on it. When we moved in it was a haven for fly tipping but I have cleared it out and planted ferns and holly bushes. The owner says he'll sell the land to me but

he has lost the ownership documents so he is having to prove to the land registry that the land is actually his. Is this true?
He 'lost' them? Perhaps. Or perhaps he doesn't really own it and is making his own claim on this unregistered land, with the intention of selling it on to you.

Can you live on it?
Yes! What type of structure you want to live in will determine if and what kind of planning permission you need.

How soon after claiming land can I build on it?
Immediately (or as long as the planning permission takes, if your structure requires it)!

Do I HAVE to live on it to make an adverse possession claim?
No you don't have to live on it, but you have to possess it - so use it for something - even if it's just camping on the weekends, or keeping a beehive, or raising animals.

Do I need to be British to claim land in the UK?
No, as long as you have regular access to the land to take care of it, your nationality is of no importance whatsoever.

I'm only 17, can I do this?
Of course you can!

Can I do this to an abandoned mine?
Yes, just be aware there might be some environmen-

tal restrictions on the land, and be very careful from a safety point of view.

Is there a limit to how big an area you can take possession of?
No, there is no limit, as long as you are using it. However, the size of the plot can affect your Permitted Development Rights (e.g. you have more Permitted Development Rights for agriculture on land larger than 5 hectares).

Is this the same as squatting?
Yes, squatting is a term often used derogatively for adverse possession.

Can I camp on it?
Of course! I know people who have claimed a small piece of land as a safe place to wild camp on with their kids.

Do I have to pay tax on it?
You are likely to be liable for a bit of tax on it, as described earlier, but the fee is negligible compared to the value of the property you obtain for free.

Is it really this easy?
Yes! It is! Now go and get yourself some land!

10. RESOURCES

Here are some links that will help you along the process of finding and claiming land.

Free map of unregistered land:
https://www.map.whoownsengland.org

Check title deeds on the government website: https://www.gov.uk/government/organisations/land-registry

UK government adverse possession guidelines:
https://www.gov.uk/government/publications/adverse-possession-of-registered-land/practice-guide-4-adverse-possession-of-registered-land

Adverse possession application form, and instructions for lodging the application:
https://www.gov.uk/government/publications/first-application-registration-fr1

11. CONCLUSION

There you have it. That is how someone of any age and any background can acquire land for free in the UK. Sure, there are some minor costs involved, such as the £3 searches for title deeds, the costs of printing a laminated sign and the cost of a fence if it isn't already fenced off, but these costs amount to next to nothing, and you get the actual plot of land completely for free. There is also the cost of your adverse possession application (£70-£130) and a small amount of tax may be due. All in all though, you are paying pennies compared to what your newly acquired land is really worth.

This process worked beautifully for me, and I have been in contact with many people for whom it has worked equally as well. All the cases I have come across of people failing in their attempts to adversely possess land have been due to their inability to follow the guidelines and requirements accurately - so attention to detail is important!

I truly hope this book has inspired you and given you the confidence to go out there and claim yourself a plot of land, knowing it is entirely legal and possible.

Once you get started, you will realise how simple the process actually is!

It is a privilege for me to be able to disseminate this information for the world to see and I hope, from the bottom of my heart, that as many of you as possible use this knowledge to improve your own lives, and the lives of those around you.

May this bring a new flavour of freedom to all!

Disclaimer

This book comprises the author's understanding from a layman's perspective of the current (June 2021) situation in England and Wales as it relates to acquiring unregistered and/or unused and/or unowned land, through the process of adverse possession. The content of the book does not constitute legal or any other kind of advice, and must not be taken as such. The author incurs no liability of any kind in respect of any claims, damages, losses, expenses or actions (legal or otherwise) resulting from any actions taken, or from any inaction, as a result of reading the book and/or of applying any of its content in practice.

Printed in Great Britain
by Amazon